PIRATES
The Secrets of Blackbeard's World

as told by
William Teach

CARLTON
KiDS

REWARD

FOR

Edward Teach,

commonly called Captain Teach, or

BLACKBEARD,

One Hundred Pounds

For every other Commander of
a Pyrate Ship, Sloop, or Vessel, ... **FORTY POUNDS**

For every Lieutenant, Master,
or Quarter-Master, Boatswain,
or Carpenter, ... **TWENTY POUNDS**

For every other inferior Officer, ... **FIFTEEN POUNDS**

And for every private Man
taken on Board such Ship,
Sloop, or Vessel,. .. .. **TEN POUNDS**

Proclamation By Alexander Spotswood,
The Governor of Virginia, November 24, 1718

CONTENTS

INTRODUCTION

It is hard to recall the moment when I first became aware of my dark heritage for it seems to me that I have always known that I am a descendant of Edward Teach, the pirate named Blackbeard.

I am neither proud nor ashamed to call this most barbarous of men my relative, though I cannot deny that the murky world he inhabited has always exerted a powerful fascination over me. I am a historian by profession, though till now I have avoided making a study of Blackbeard – it is as if I feared that by looking too closely into this man's devilish life I might discover in myself a heart as black as his. However, a few years ago events took a most mysterious turn...

One icy morning in late November a mysterious package was delivered to my front door. There was no return address, though I was just able to make out a London postmark. Upon opening the package, I was astonished to find a weather-beaten oilskin tied up with string and an envelope on which my name was written in a strange, old-fashioned hand. Trembling, for a terrible sense of foreboding had crept over me, I found a note signed from one Benjamin Hands:

My time is near. These things should be, and always should have been, yours. They have brought me no peace, I trust it will not be so with you.

Anxiously, I untied the oilskin and was at once struck by the musky odour that arose from its decaying interior. There I found a pistol wrapped in a stained cloth, a braid of jet-black hair tied with a fraying cord, an ornate compass and a small battered purse, out of which tumbled four gold coins. Most intriguingly of all, there was a torn page with some rough markings and the words "Hell's Cove" faintly scrawled across it.

My blood ran cold. The name "Hands" now reverberated in my head, for I knew Israel Hands had been Blackbeard's first mate. Tried after Blackbeard's death, Israel escaped the hangman's noose – it is claimed he testified against the members of his former crew in exchange for a pardon. Nobody knows what happened to Israel, though some say he ended his days begging on the streets of London.

As for the items sent to me, the age of the pistol has been verified as early eighteenth century, the compass mid-seventeenth century, and the gold coins are French, dating from the reign of Louis XIV. A research of public records has failed to throw up a Benjamin Hands of any significance and there is no known place in North Carolina, or elsewhere, by the name of Hell's Cove. The evidence is by no means clear cut and some will doubt my reasoning, yet my every instinct leads me to conclude that the objects – shown in this book for the first time – belonged to none other than Blackbeard. How Israel Hands came to be in possession of them, how he kept them hidden during his imprisonment, or who Benjamin Hands is, well, that is for the reader to decide.

William Teach,
OXFORD

My time is near.

These things should be, and always should have been, yours.

They have brought me no peace, I trust it will not be so with you.

Benjamin Hands

Hell's Cove

A NOTE FROM THE PUBLISHER

It is a great sadness that as we go to press, William Teach has been missing for close to two years. Upon finishing his manuscript, Mr Teach, no doubt inspired by his research and spurred on by the curious note sent to him by Benjamin Hands, felt compelled to visit the region in which his ancestor Blackbeard operated. The strange circumstances surrounding William Teach's disappearance have been much publicized - since the last known sighting of him on Ocracoke Island, the police investigation has drawn a blank. We remain hopeful of a positive outcome, but now feel it is in the public interest to proceed with publication of this book. We would like to pay tribute to William Teach, a fine scholar and valued friend and colleague.

BLACKBEARD'S WORLD

THE YEAR IS 1717. AS DUSK FALLS ON A DECEMBER EVENING, THE *GYPSY* - A SLAVE SHIP LADEN WITH SUGAR AND RUM - CUTS THROUGH THE WARM WATERS OF THE BAHAMAS CHANNEL.

On the horizon, the lookout spots a three-masted square-rigger and a sloop flying the British Union flag. As the vessels draw close, the colours are suddenly dropped, and the dreaded Jolly Roger is swiftly hoisted up. The crack of a gunshot fired across the bows of the *Gypsy* shatters the quiet, and bloodthirsty cries fill the air. Resistance against the pirates is futile. The slave ship lowers her sails and heaves to.

The *Gypsy*'s captain is ordered to board the pirate vessel: "Come on up, ye scurvy dog!" On deck, the trembling man is confronted by a towering figure with long braided hair and a jet-black beard. A sash stuffed with pistols is slung around his enormous chest and his cutlass glints in the dying light. Cold terror clutches the captain as he meets the pirate's devilish gaze, for the wild and savage eyes belong to none other than Blackbeard...

CURSE

❧ of the ❧

CARIBBEAN

PIRATES HAVE EXISTED AS LONG AS MEN HAVE ROAMED THE SEAS, BUT ONE BRIEF PERIOD EXTENDING FROM 1690 TO 1730 IS KNOWN AS THE GOLDEN AGE OF

PIRACY

This was Blackbeard's era.

A lawless age when he and other scurrilous rogues such as Bartholomew Roberts and Edward Low spread terror across the waters of the Caribbean and along the East coast of North America.

A Pirate's Life for Me

A pirate's life was nearly always short and brutal, but pirating promised the possibility of freedom and untold riches. When the War of the Spanish Succession ended in 1714, many seamen and former privateers – men permitted by their governments to attack foreign shipping – were left unemployed and the lure of piracy was strong.

The absence of strong government in the Caribbean and the American colonies created an ideal hunting ground for pirates, and the pickings were rich. Merchant ships carried valuable trade goods, and slave ships sailing from Africa were laden with rum and sugar from the Caribbean.

The End of an Era

The black-market trade between pirates and the inhabitants of the American colonies was for a time largely overlooked by colonial governors. However, as the danger to shipping became too great to ignore, these same governors turned to ruthlessly hunting down the pirates. Many cutthroats, Blackbeard included, met gruesome ends as justice finally caught up with them.

IT IS SAID, THOUGH, THAT THEIR SPIRITS LIVE ON – FOR THOSE WHO HAVE NO FEAR OF DEATH, AND WHO LIVE AND DIE BY THE CUTLASS, CAN NEVER BE FULLY CONQUERED...

ATLANTIC OR WESTERN OCEAN

MAP of the WEST INDIES during the GOLDEN AGE of PIRACY

Bermudas Is

BAHAMA ISLANDS

Lucayos
Eleuthera
Providence
Cat I.
Watling
Long I.
d Bank
Crooked I.
Maguana
Atwoods Keys
Caicos Is
Tropic of Cancer
Inagua I.

CARIBBEE

Windward
Tortuga I.
Mont Christo
S. Jago
C. Francois
Scots B.
Samana I.
S. Jago
C. Mays
C. S. Nicolas
St Anns Harbour
P. d Guanives
HISPANIOLA or St DOMINGO
C del Engano
S. Domingo
Saona I.
Mona
Sta Cruz F.
PORTO RICO
Porto Rico
Virgin Is
Saba
Anegeda
Anguilla E.
S. Martin S.F.
S. Barthe Comen F.
Barbuda E.
Kingston
Petit Guava's
C. Tiburon
Piche I.
P. Louis
P. ta Hermosa
C Alta
Leeward
Eustatia D.
S. Kits E.
Nevis
Antego E.
Redonda E.
Montserrat E.
Doseada F.
Guadalupe E.
Margalante
Dominica E.
Avis
JAMAICA
Navasa I.
Port Royal
P. Morant
Antilles

CARIBBEAN SEA

Windward Islands
Martinico E.
S. Lucia N.
Barbadoes E.
S Vincent N.

Little Antilles
Galleons from Old Spain
C Conquibacoa
C de la Vela
Aruba
Curasao
Bonaire
Aves I.
Roca
Orchilla
Blanco
Cartagena
Grenadillos
Grenada F.
Tobago N.
The Track
P. Samba
P. Canoa
S. Martha
R. de la Hache
Maracaybo
Coro
Lake
Maracaybo
Tartuga
Triest
Guaira
Margarita
C Galera
Trinidad
Cartagene
chica
Keys
Mopox
los Reyes
CARACOS
Caracos
Comana
Verina
G. of Paria
CARTAGENA
Truxillo
NEW
Oronoque Is & R.
Hocomoco P
C Nassau
TERRA FIRMA
Merida
VENEZUELA
ANDALUSIA
Ariacoa
GUIANA
R. Esquebe
Sta Fee
Apuerto
New Segovia
N. Middleburg
Look about
NEW GRANADA
Pamplona
Truxillo
S. Thomas
El Desembarcadero
Velez
Caripa
SOUTH AMERICA

Blackbeard

IN BLACKBEARD'S TIME the mere mention of this villain's name was enough to make sailors quake with dread. Bartholomew Roberts captured more ships, Henry Avery took more treasure and Edward Low was crueller by far - and yet it is the murderous Blackbeard that lives on in our darkest dreams. What, then, do we know of this man once described as "so fierce and wild... that imagination cannot form an idea of a Fury, from Hell, to look more frightful"?

Blackbeard Goes a-Pirating

Blackbeard was the name given to Edward Teach, a seaman born in Bristol, England. He started his career aboard a British privateer - a ship permitted to attack foreign vessels - but when peace came in 1714 he made for New Providence, a notorious pirate haven in the Bahamas. Here he joined the crew of Benjamin Hornigold and by 1716 was in charge of his own sloop. In November 1717 he captured a slave ship - renaming her the *Queen Anne's Revenge* - and had her fitted out with 40 large guns. By early 1718, Blackbeard had four vessels under his command and had established a hideout on Ocracoke Island in North Carolina - a base from where he and his pirates plundered at will.

The Nature of the Beast

Blackbeard's ferocious appearance was a truly powerful weapon. Tall and lean, he had a long black beard that covered most of his face. In battle he wore a sling with three brace of pistols hanging in holsters, and was said to fix lighted matches under his hat. His wild and staring eyes horrified even his own crew who came to believe he was the devil himself.

TO
HELL & BACK

It is told that
BLACKBEARD
once challenged his men with these words:

"Come, let us make a Hell of our own, and try how long we can bear it".

He and some of his crew went into the ship's hold and after closing all the hatches filled several pots with brimstone and set them on fire. Ignoring his men's gasps for air, Blackbeard only opened the hatches when his near-lifeless men were on the point of suffocation.

BLACKBEARD

Blackbeard lights brimstone to test how long he and his men can bear the suffocating fumes.

Be Ye Warned!

It is said that Blackbeard was courteous to those who surrendered and merciless to those who did not. The chilling message contained in his macabre flag could hardly be clearer. A devil-horned skeleton holding an hourglass warns that time is running out for the victim, while the bleeding heart signals that resistance will surely result in certain death.

SAILING *the* HIGH SEAS

IT IS FEBRUARY 1718 AND A THREE-MASTED SQUARE RIGGER PLOUGHS THROUGH THE ROUGH SEA JUST OFF ST CHRISTOPHER ISLAND IN THE WEST INDIES.

At first glance she looks like any other merchantman plying these waters, but this is no ordinary vessel – for the ship is equipped with 40 guns and crammed with 300 villainous rogues ready to fight to the death. As dangerous as any warship, she is none other than Blackbeard's vessel, the *Queen Anne's Revenge*.

Most pirate ships were much smaller than Blackbeard's imposing flagship, but shared several features in common. They needed to be well armed, and swift enough to overcome their prey or evade capture. Pirate ships also needed to be extremely seaworthy – they travelled vast distances, and were often exposed to wild and stormy seas and hurricane-strength winds. Many were the ships that ended up dashed on rocks or claimed by the unforgiving sea...

Pirate Ships

WHAT IS A PIRATE WITHOUT A SHIP? From the simple sloop to the formidable warship, pirate vessels came in many guises and were the pirate's lifeblood, providing shelter and a powerful weapon of intimidation. It was the nature of the business that pirates acquired their ships through foul means, either mutiny or theft, and adapted them to suit their evil ends. Once a pirate had taken his first ship, he could trade this in for a bigger and better prize when the opportunity arose.

The Sloop

Valued for its lightning speed and nimbleness, this vessel was a small, single-masted ship with a top speed of 10 knots. The sloop could carry up to 70 pirates and because she had a shallow draft – meaning the keel was not far below the waterline – she could swiftly be moved inland when danger threatened.

A CRIME OF
OPPORTUNITY

Although pirates favoured certain types of ship, ultimately any vessel might do.

EDWARD LOW

started his career serving aboard a British sloop. Following an argument with the ship's captain just off the coast of Honduras, Low and several of his crew mates made off in the ship's small boat determined to conquer the seas.

As Charles Johnson put it in 1724:

"The next day they took a small vessel, and go in her, make a black flag, and declare war against all the world."

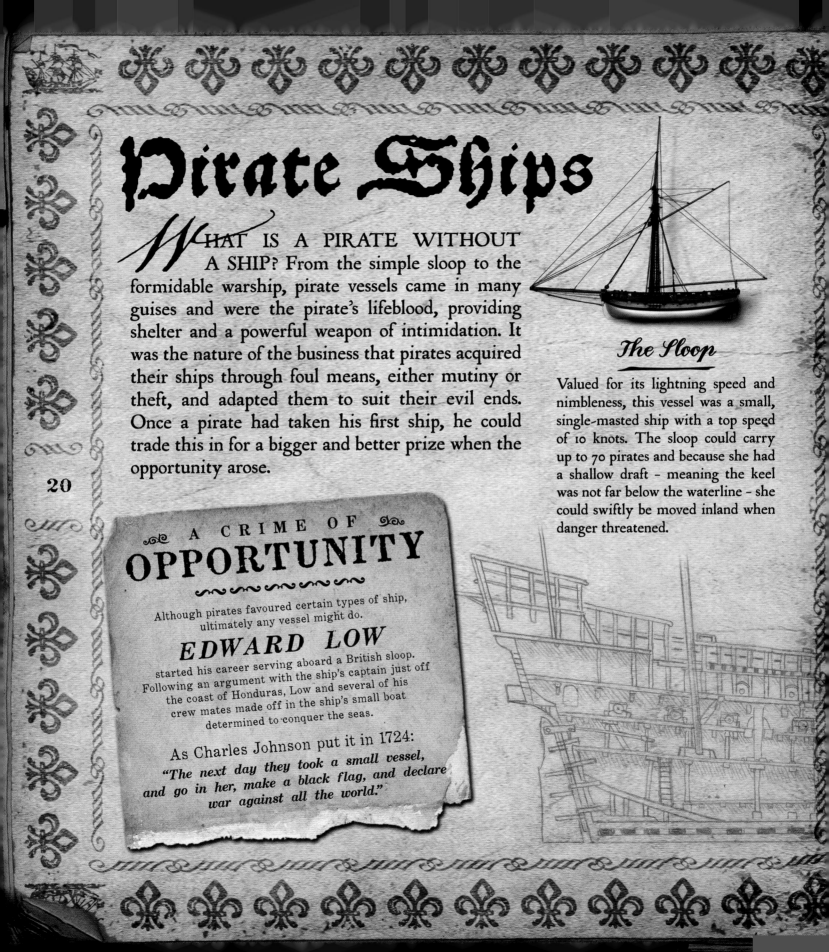

The Schooner

Sleek and swift, this small American vessel provided a superb means of running down prey. With two masts, she had an even shallower draft than the sloop and could carry up to 75 men.

The Brigantine

Heavier and longer than the sloop or schooner, the two-masted brigantine still had terrific speed. Carrying up to 12 guns, this sturdy vessel fared well in prolonged battles and could carry up to 90 men.

The Square Rigger

Pirates frequently attacked these large, three-masted vessels for they were often laden with valuable trade goods. They were slower and less agile than smaller pirate vessels, but could be turned into huge floating fortresses, as in the case of the *Queen Anne's Revenge*.

THE QUEEN ANNE'S REVENGE

❧❧❧❧❧❧❧❧❧❧❧

BLACKBEARD'S commanding flagship almost certainly began life as the *Concorde*, a 14-gun French merchantman and later a slave ship. Upon capturing this powerful vessel, Blackbeard immediately set about converting her to suit his wicked ends. Additional gunports were cut in her sides and her weapons increased to 40 guns. The ship's forecastle was cut down to create an open area upon which the pirates could freely fight, and where slaves had once been secreted away below deck, there was plenty of room to hide a large crew of murderous cutthroats.

THE CAPTAIN'S CABIN

No Quarter Given

There could be few more troubling sights for any sailor than that of the dreaded Jolly Roger. Intended to spread mortal terror, pirate flags featured grim symbols of death: skeletons, cutlasses, daggers and bleeding hearts. Their message was clear: no quarter – mercy – would be given or expected in return.

The Nature of the Beast

THE NAME "Jolly Roger" is believed to have come from the French *joli rouge*, meaning "pretty red" - the mocking name given to the blood-red banners flown by earlier pirates. Others say that "Old Roger" was a name for the devil himself, and that the "jolly" referred to the apparent grin of a skull. By the early 1700s, pirate captains had begun to fly their own personal flags, and by Blackbeard's time these chilling banners of death had become an all too familiar sight across the Caribbean.

 JACK RACKHAM

Crossed cutlasses take the place of crossed bones in Jack Rackham's menacing flag.

STEDE BONNET

The scales of pirate justice are represented in Stede Bonnet's ghoulish flag, with a dagger signifying death on one side of the skull and a heart to stand for life on the other.

BARTHOLOMEW ROBERTS

The alarming threat contained in Bartholomew Robert's flag is unmistakable - the pirate depicts himself as a fearless fighter, two skulls crushed beneath his feet.

Jack Rackham

The dark tale of Jack Rackham and his bloodthirsty female accomplices, Anne Bonny and Mary Read – two cutthroats who fought as bravely as any man – is a curious one of trickery, treachery and intrigue.

IN 1718, "CALICO" JACK RACKHAM – so known for his colourful clothes – was a small-time pirate captain. In 1719 he sought and received a pardon from Woodes Rogers, the governor of New Providence. It was here that Rackham met and fell in love with Anne Bonny. However, Rackham soon tired of life on land, and the pirate returned to his evil ways, this time accompanied by Bonny.

Mary Read was born in London and raised as a boy to ensure an inheritance. As a teenager, and still disguised as a man, she joined the navy and boarded a vessel for the West Indies. It seems Rackham attacked this ship and Mary joined his crew. For over a year this odd group cruised off the coast of Cuba, where. Bonny and Read, "as fierce as hellcats", became known for their ferocious fighting practices.

Hanged like Dogs

In 1720, Rackham's ship was anchored off the western tip of Jamaica when a government sloop took the pirates by surprise. The men were drunk after a night's carousing and hid below deck, leaving the women to defend the ship. Anne and Mary fought valiantly, but all were captured and taken to stand trial in Jamaica.

Calico Jack and the male crew members were sentenced to hang. Anne Bonny was allowed to see Rackham before his execution – her scathing words to him echo down the centuries: "Had you fought like a man, you need not have been hang'd like a dog!" Read and Bonny were also found guilty but, being pregnant, both escaped the hangman's noose. What became of these shameless tricksters, no one can be sure.

28

Anne Bonny and Mary Read

THE
TRYALS
OF
Captain John Rackam,
AND OTHER
PIRATES, Viz

Geroge Fetherston,
Richard Corner,
John Davies,
John Howell,
Tho.Bourn, alias Brown,

Noah Hardwood,
James Dobbins,
Patrick Carty,
Thomas Earl,
John Fenwick, al'Fenis

Who were all Condemn'd for PIRACY, at the Town of St. Jago de la Vega, in the Island of JAMAICA, on Wednesday and Thursday the Sixteenth and Seventeenth Days of November 1720.

AS ALSO, THE
TRYALS of Mary Read and Anne Bonny, alias Bonn, on Monday the 28th Day of the said Month of November, at St. Jago de le Vega aforesaid.

And of several Others, who were also condemn'd for PIRACY.

ALSO,
A True Copy of the Act of Parliament made for the more effectual Suppression of Piracy.

Jamaica: Printed by Robert Baldwin, in the Year 1721.

BROUGHT TO ACCOUNT
The title page from a bestselling sensational pamphlet, which was published in 1721.

Dead Reckoning

THE SPYGLASS

The spyglass, a hand-held telescope, was vital for spotting distant prizes. It also allowed the navigator to plot a course by studying landmarks and the heavens above. Looking at the sun through a spyglass was never advisable. Many were the seamen who lost the use of an eye - and gained an eye patch - thus!

THE CARIBBEAN and the east coast of North America were vast and treacherous waters for the inexperienced mariner. At the turn of the eighteenth century, navigational instruments were still crude. A pirate captain therefore had to rely on exceptional seamanship and a large degree of "dead reckoning" – an instinctive sense of direction and a fair amount of guesswork – to ensure he found his prizes and lived to tell the tale.

THE COMPASS

The most important instrument for determining direction was the compass. Mounted on a rotating ring or gimbals, the compass could be kept level no matter how much a ship was listing. With the magnetic needle pointing north, the navigator could thus determine the vessel's course.

What voyages has this compass needle directed? And could it be that Blackbeard used this very device to navigate the high seas? If so, it is almost certain the pirate stole this ornate treasure from one of the many ships he plundered. W. Teach.

SEA CHARTS

Essential for any long voyage, printed sea charts provided important information concerning sea depth, and gave warning of concealed reefs and rocks. Any pirate captain would almost certainly have relied, too, on his own charts and rough logbook notes to steer through familiar territory.

AT A RATE OF KNOTS

Measuring the speed at which a ship was travelling was an important part of a captain's dead reckoning. A seaman would throw an anchor from the stern allowing its rope to play out freely for around 30 seconds. The rope would have knots tied at regular intervals; by counting how many knots crossed the stern in a given time, an estimate of the ship's speed could be calculated.

❧ THE ❧
BACKSTAFF

This vital instrument
CALCULATED LATITUDE
at sea - an angular measurement
north or south from the equator - by measuring
the sun's height at midday.

*There would be no reliable instrument to measure
longitude - one's position east or west - until 1773.*

A PIRATE'S LIFE

IT IS EARLY 1718 AND A STORM HOWLS ACROSS THE CARIBBEAN. JUST OFF THE WESTERN COAST OF ST VINCENT THE *QUEEN ANNE'S REVENGE* LISTS HORRIBLY ON THE RAGING SEA.

Belowdecks all is dark. Blackbeard's men lie tightly crammed on the floor, while those in hammocks sway in continual motion. Seawater periodically slops down the hatchways and damp penetrates everything. The air is unbearably hot and the stench of 300 unwashed bodies mingles with that of rotting fish and foul bilge water. Rats can be heard scuttling past the men's heads and cockroaches lurk in every crack and corner...

What man would choose such a life – one that if it were not cut short by disease or injury, would almost certainly end at the gallows? At a time when grinding poverty was commonplace, and harsh punishments were dealt out for the slightest offence, a life of piracy was seen as one freely chosen. A pirate weighed up his experience of life against the promise of unimaginable wealth – and choosing the latter, laughed in the face of death.

Life on Board

Conditions aboard a pirate vessel could be very harsh. Living quarters were horribly cramped and dirty, food and water turned foul, rats and cockroaches brought misery, and infectious illnesses spread like wildfire. The thrill of the chase or the excitement of battle were only a small part of the many long weeks at sea – like other sailors of the age, pirates had to endure an endless round of hard physical labour.

✋ SHIP'S BISCUIT
"Hard tack" biscuits could last for up to a year and provided the main food on long voyages. However, they were still likely to be infested with tiny maggot-like creatures called weevils.

A Crew of Villains

Almost all pirates were experienced sailors, and many of the jobs to be done on board were the same as on any other ship. The *captain* was elected by the crew, chosen for his seamanship and ruthless daring in the heat of battle.

The *quartermaster* or *first mate* was second in command, and saw to the day-to-day running of the ship, making sure the rules were obeyed. The *boatswain* (bosun) was a junior officer whose responsibilities included ensuring the ship was in seaworthy condition. A ship's *gunner* was in charge of the cannon - accuracy in aiming was a skill that took many years to perfect. The vital role of looking after the ship's wooden parts fell to the *carpenter* who repaired any damaged timbers and plugged leaky holes. The *cook* looked after the food stores, preparing meals from the basic ingredients to hand. The most junior crew member was the *cabin boy*, who scrubbed the decks and carried out other lowly tasks.

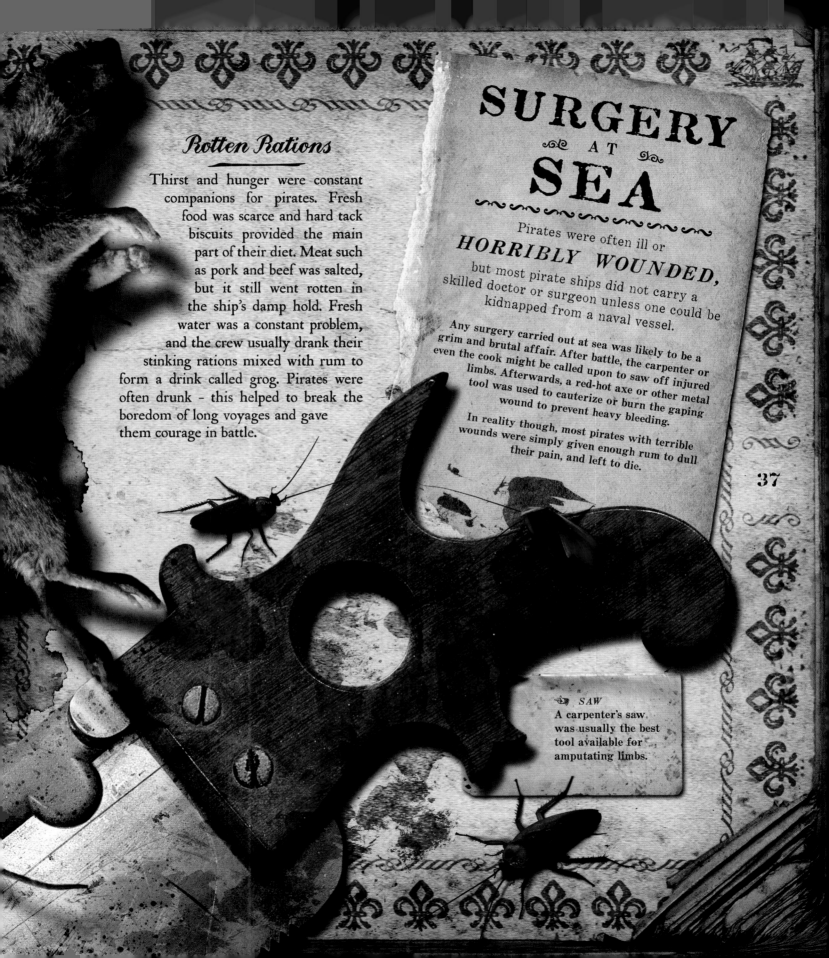

Rotten Rations

Thirst and hunger were constant companions for pirates. Fresh food was scarce and hard tack biscuits provided the main part of their diet. Meat such as pork and beef was salted, but it still went rotten in the ship's damp hold. Fresh water was a constant problem, and the crew usually drank their stinking rations mixed with rum to form a drink called grog. Pirates were often drunk - this helped to break the boredom of long voyages and gave them courage in battle.

SURGERY AT SEA

Pirates were often ill or **HORRIBLY WOUNDED,** but most pirate ships did not carry a skilled doctor or surgeon unless one could be kidnapped from a naval vessel.

Any surgery carried out at sea was likely to be a grim and brutal affair. After battle, the carpenter or even the cook might be called upon to saw off injured limbs. Afterwards, a red-hot axe or other metal tool was used to cauterize or burn the gaping wound to prevent heavy bleeding.

In reality though, most pirates with terrible wounds were simply given enough rum to dull their pain, and left to die.

SAW
A carpenter's saw was usually the best tool available for amputating limbs.

Bartholomew Roberts

Perhaps the most successful raider ever to sail the high seas, the dashing "Black Bart" – who drank tea instead of rum and never killed on the Sabbath – captured over 400 ships in less than three years.

IN 1719, ROBERTS WAS FORCED to turn pirate when the cutthroat Howell Davis captured the slave ship on which he was serving. Only a month later Davis was killed and the crew, impressed by Robert's extreme cunning, elected him Captain. And so began Black Bart's deadly spree of terror...

Sailing first for Brazil, Roberts captured several Portuguese ships before making for the waters of Newfoundland where he wreaked havoc along the coast. In September 1720, the pirate started a furious rampage through the Caribbean. One of the prizes he captured was a 52-gun warship. On board was the governor of Martinique – Roberts hanged him from the yardam of his ship before torturing and murdering the crew. He then set about converting this vessel, renamed the *Royal Fortune*, into a powerful ship of terror.

Tossed to the Hungry Sea

Black Bart's murderous career finally came to an end in February 1722. After a night of merry-making he and his crew were at anchor off Cape Lopez on the West African coast. As dawn broke, the British warship HMS *Swallow* took them by surprise. Roberts made an attempt to escape, but was stopped by grapeshot fired at close range. When the smoke cleared, the pirate, dressed in fine crimson and with a diamond-studded cross about his neck, lay dead on the deck. His men swiftly threw his bloody body overboard before finally surrendering themselves. Their fate was no less dreadful – after the largest pirate trial ever held, 54 of the 264 pirates captured were sent to the gallows.

39

A Life of Rum

—Such a Day, Rum all out: —
Our Company somewhat sober:
— A damn'd Confusion amongst
us! — Rogues a plotting; —great
Talk of Separation. — So I look'd
sharp for a Prize; — Such a
Day took one, with a great deal
of Liquor on Board, so kept the
Company hot, damned hot, then all
Things went well again.

AN EXTRACT FROM
BLACKBEARD'S JOURNAL

Pirate Articles

Although pirates were outlaws, men who answered to nobody but themselves, their ships were often governed by a code of conduct. Each crew member was required to sign a set of "articles" before swearing an oath of allegiance on the Bible, or perhaps upon crossed pistols or a human skull.

No Prey, No Pay

The pirate captain was elected by the crew and could be voted out at any point. Although pirates received no wages, when a ship was captured the booty was divided among them. Wounded crew members were often compensated for their injuries according to a scale - losing a limb would be worth more money than the loss of an eye, for example. The articles also made clear the price that would be paid if the rules were broken. For Bartholomew Robert's crew, deserting the ship in battle would result in one of the worst pirate punishments of all - a slow and terrible death marooned on a desert island.

THE ARTICLES OF
BARTHOLOMEW ROBERTS

ARTICLE I

Every man shall have an equal vote in affairs of moment. He shall have an equal title to the fresh provisions or strong liquors at any time seized, and shall use them at pleasure unless a scarcity may make it necessary for the common good that a retrenchment may be voted.

ARTICLE II

Every man shall be called fairly in turn by the list on board of prizes, because over and above their proper share, they are allowed a shift of clothes. But if they defraud the company to the value of even one dollar in plate, jewels or money, they shall be marooned. If any man rob another he shall have his nose and ears slit, and be put ashore where he shall be sure to encounter hardships.

ARTICLE III

None shall game for money either with dice or cards.

ARTICLE IV

The lights and candles should be put out at eight at night, and if any of the crew desire to drink after that hour they shall sit upon the open deck without lights.

ARTICLE V

Each man shall keep his piece, cutlass and pistols at all times clean and ready for action.

ARTICLE VI

No boy or woman to be allowed amongst them. If any man shall be found seducing any of the latter sex and carrying her to sea in disguise he shall suffer death.

ARTICLE VII

He that shall desert the ship or his quarters in time of battle shall be punished by death or marooning.

ARTICLE VIII

None shall strike another on board the ship, but every man's quarrel shall be ended on shore by sword or pistol in this manner. At the word of command from the quartermaster, each man being previously placed back to back, shall turn and fire immediately. If any man do not, the quartermaster shall knock the piece out of his hand. If both miss their aim they shall take to their cutlasses, and he that draweth first blood shall be declared the victor.

ARTICLE IX

No man shall talk of breaking up their way of living till each has a share of 1,000. Every man who shall become a cripple or lose a limb in the service shall have 800 pieces of eight from the common stock and for lesser hurts proportionately.

ARTICLE X

The captain and the quartermaster shall each receive two shares of a prize, the master gunner and boatswain, one and one half shares, all other officers one and one quarter, and private gentlemen of fortune one share each.

ARTICLE XI

The musicians shall have rest on the Sabbath Day only by right. On all other days by favour only.

Punishments and Torture

Pirates were almost all rough seamen, capable of dreadful acts of cruelty. Torture was a means of extracting information from prisoners and very effective in spreading terror. Vicious punishments were also turned on pirate crew members – those who disobeyed the ship's articles might find themselves clapped in irons, keelhauled or, worst of all, marooned on a desert island.

Walking the Plank

Walking the plank - where a victim was weighed down, blindfolded and then forced to walk off a plank into the sea depths - may have occurred on some ships, though most pirates would have found this too troublesome a ritual to carry out. When necessary, it was quicker and easier to simply throw a man overboard...

THE CAT O' NINE TAILS

An especially nasty whip made of cow or horse hide, the cat had nine knotted "tails" and was frequently used for whippings on naval vessels. It was less common on pirate ships, as many pirates were former navy men and rejected the brutal discipline of their old lives. However, captured pirates might well have found themselves at the mercy of a savage flogging.

Woolding

This sickening form of torture involved tying a short length of rope around the victim's head. The ends were attached to a block of wood that was turned to inflict ever-increasing pressure around the temples, causing the eyes to eventually bulge out of their sockets.

Being Clapped in Irons

A pirate could be punished or a prisoner forced to reveal secrets by having their hands and legs locked in iron chains or tightly bound with rope. The punishment could be intensified by leaving the victim out on deck to be scorched by the sun, or lashed by wind and rain.

Sweating

This was a particularly humiliating form of punishment, where the victim was forced to run around the mainmast while pirates pricked and prodded him with cutlasses from all sides.

Keelhauling

The ghastly punishment of keelhauling usually resulted in death. The victim would be tied to a rope that looped under the vessel before being dragged underneath the ship from one side to the other. If he didn't drown, then the victim would likely die from wounds inflicted by razor-sharp barnacles on the ship's keel.

Marooning

This punishment was reserved for the worst of crimes – cheating one's fellow pirates or cowardice in battle. The victim was left on a desert island, perhaps with a pistol and one round of shot – he was then free to take his own life rather than endure the long and lonely wait for death through starvation.

45

Israel Hands

Little is known of Israel Hands, Blackbeard's trusted first mate. There are no records of his early piratical career but he must have been an able leader of men, for in March 1718 Blackbeard gave him command of the captured 10-gun sloop Adventure.

HANDS SERVED HIS CAPTAIN till the end – an astonishing fact when we learn that his crippling limp was the result of an injury inflicted by Blackbeard himself. But history cannot tell us all – for who can know what sharpened daggers lay hidden in Israel Hands' heart?

Dicing With the Devil

The story is told of how one night Blackbeard was drinking and playing cards in his cabin with Israel, and two other members of crew. During the game, the captain slyly drew out two pistols, keeping them hidden under the table. This action was observed by one of the sailors – terrified, he made his excuses and swiftly left the cabin. Upon the man's departure, Blackbeard blew out the candles. After a few seconds, two shots cracked through the air. Israel Hands screamed out in the darkness, for one of the bullets had shattered his knee.

Hands, undoubtedly lamed for life, later asked Blackbeard the meaning of his act. The captain only answered that if he did not kill one of his men now and then, they would forget who he was. It is hard to imagine that Israel – who some say ended his life begging on the streets of London – ever forgot Blackbeard or his dreadful act of treachery.

Is this one of the six pistols that
Blackbeard wore slung around his
body, perhaps the very weapon that
crippled Israel Hands? It is astonishing to
think that Blackbeard's powerful hand may
once have gripped its handle, or to imagine
what terrible scenes have unfolded
in its presence... W. Teach.

New Providence

For a few years in the early eighteenth century, New Providence, a small island in the centre of the Bahamas, was the base for hundreds of pirates. The most notorious rogues of the age flocked to this wild and lawless place – villains such as Blackbeard, Jack Rackham and Samuel Bellamy all found a welcome at Nassau, the island's main settlement. Here they could sell their loot, refit their ships, and make merry in the many taverns and gambling dens.

Beyond the Reach of the Law

There were very few places where pirates could safely come ashore to make vital repairs, take on supplies or shelter from ferocious storms. Wherever these cutthroats sailed the seas, so too they established land hideouts where they could take cover. During Blackbeard's era, New Providence was the largest such haven in the Americas. Close to shipping routes, it had no governor, a plentiful supply of food and water, high hills to provide lookout points and a harbour too shallow for naval warships. After months at sea, pirates craved the paradise that New Providence seemed to offer.

However, there were dangers lurking in Nassau's rowdy drinking dens and dark alleys - for robbers and murderers found easy prey in a place where money and liquor flowed in equal measure. Some of the pirates who came ashore at New Providence disappeared, never to be seen again...

A Pirate's Paradise Destroyed

In 1718, the British government decided it was time to restore authority and appointed Woodes Rogers as governor of New Providence. When Rogers arrived escorted by three naval warships, most pirates fled, while others gave up their way of life in exchange for a pardon. A mass hanging of pirates in December 1718 proved that the new governor was taking his role seriously - New Providence's wild piratical days had come to an end.

PIRATE ATTACK

THE SEA IS DEADLY CALM BUT THE AIR IS FRAUGHT WITH DANGER. A MERCHANT SHIP NAMED THE *REGENT* HAS IGNORED A WARNING BLAST FROM THE *QUEEN ANNE'S REVENGE* AND THE CHASE IS ON.

Hastily, the pirates throw sand on the decks to prevent them becoming slippery with blood and the hatches are shut tight so no man can escape belowdecks. A marksman fires at the *Regent*'s crew – her helmsman drops dead and the ship veers wildly off course. Blackbeard's men draw level with their prey and pull the vessel close with grappling hooks. Screaming threats and swinging their cutlasses, the pirates swarm aboard.

Pirates aimed to terrify their victims into surrender rather than risk damaging a prize in battle. Most sailors offered little resistance when confronted with the sight of the Jolly Roger. If a ship did try to flee, then pirates used their cannon to fire shrapnel to maim and kill, while chain shot was used to bring down rigging and masts. Once the pirates had boarded a vessel, brutal hand-to-hand combat could begin...

～ FIRING A ～
BROADSIDE

To discharge all the guns from one side of a ship at once was known as firing a broadside. A ship's large cannon were mounted on four-wheeled bases and required several highly skilled men to operate them correctly.

Surrounded by the deafening roar of cannonfire, pirate gunners needed to remain calm and focused in the heat of battle. Chainshot and barshot were used to bring down rigging and sails, while roundshot (cannonballs) and grapeshot could be used to cut down men on the deck.

Great expertise was needed to avoid badly damaging or sinking a ship, the pirates' prize.

Blackbeard Blockades Charleston

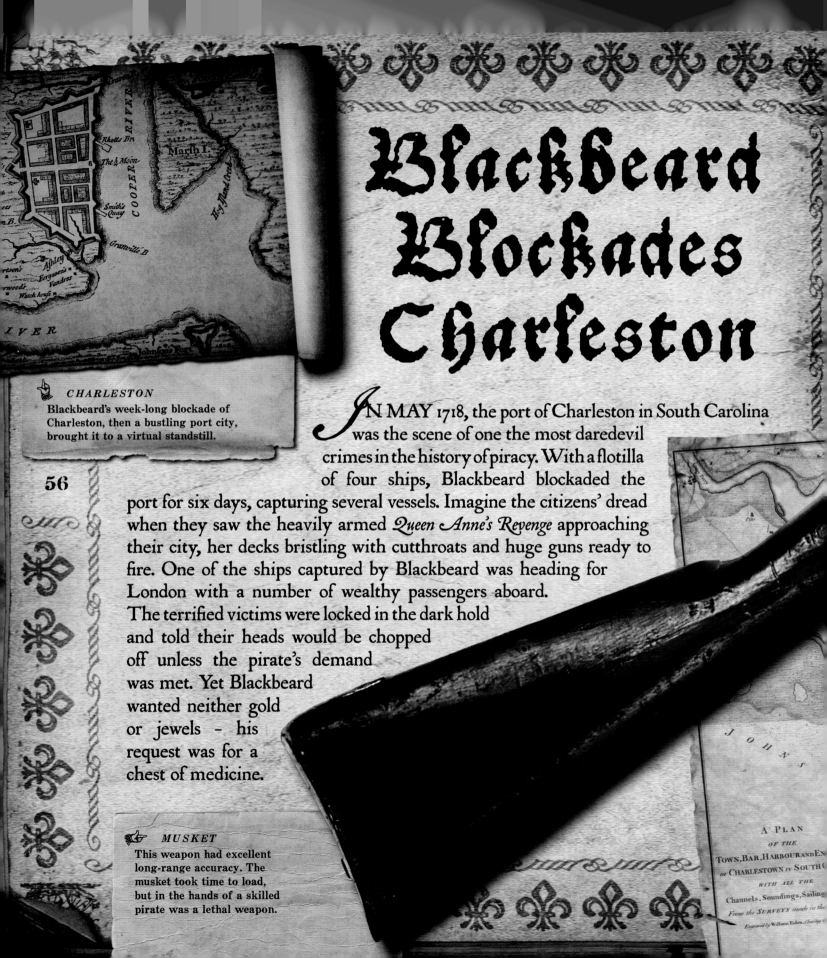

CHARLESTON

Blackbeard's week-long blockade of Charleston, then a bustling port city, brought it to a virtual standstill.

IN MAY 1718, the port of Charleston in South Carolina was the scene of one the most daredevil crimes in the history of piracy. With a flotilla of four ships, Blackbeard blockaded the port for six days, capturing several vessels. Imagine the citizens' dread when they saw the heavily armed *Queen Anne's Revenge* approaching their city, her decks bristling with cutthroats and huge guns ready to fire. One of the ships captured by Blackbeard was heading for London with a number of wealthy passengers aboard. The terrified victims were locked in the dark hold and told their heads would be chopped off unless the pirate's demand was met. Yet Blackbeard wanted neither gold or jewels – his request was for a chest of medicine.

MUSKET

This weapon had excellent long-range accuracy. The musket took time to load, but in the hands of a skilled pirate was a lethal weapon.

A PLAN OF THE TOWN, BAR, HARBOUR AND ENTRANCE of CHARLESTOWN IN SOUTH C
WITH ALL THE
Channels, Soundings, Sailing
From the SURVEYS made in the
Engraved by William Faden, Charing C

Off With Their Heads!

A few pirates and one hostage were sent in a boat to inform Charleston's governor of Blackbeard's demand. After two days had passed with no sign of the boat's return, the terrified prisoners were told to prepare for death. When a messenger arrived to beg for more time, Blackbeard granted a further two days but still the medicines did not appear. As the pirates moved their ships into the harbour, panic spread throughout the city. Finally, the boat appeared in the distance, the medicine chest on board. Blackbeard released the ships and his petrified hostages, though not before stripping them of their clothes and finery.

BLACKBEARD'S MEN
Pirates, with muskets slung over their shoulders, boldly march through Charleston.

57

A PIRATE'S ARSENAL

In most cases the mere sight of
THE BLACK FLAG
or the bloodthirsty cries of a well-armed pirate crew were enough
to cause a ship's captain to surrender. However, when a bloodless
victory proved impossible, pirates preferred to fight their victims
up close rather than using their ship's guns from a distance. This
ensured they did as little damage as possible to the ship they
wished to capture or her precious cargo.

*Human life was of little value and pirates used a variety of
hand weapons to skilfully cut down their opponents on deck.*

CUTLASS
The most popular
sword used by pirates
was the cutlass. With a short
curved blade, it was very effective at
close quarters and could be used to slash
through a crowded deck of men. It was
also useful as a boarding tool, and could
slice through heavy ropes and canvas.

BOARDING AXE

Boarding axes were used to help pirates scale the sides of a ship and cut through rigging. As a crew moved to plunder a vessel, the axe could be used to hack down doors, hatches or anything else that stood in the pirates' way.

BLUNDERBUSS

Highly effective at close range, the deadly blunderbuss could scatter a spray of lead shot over a wide area, causing horrific carnage in a single shot.

DAGGER

Daggers and other small knives were used in desperate hand-to-hand combat. A thrusting weapon for inflicting deep stab wounds, the dagger was the last line of defence in battle.

GRENADO

Made of iron, glass or wood, this small grenade was filled with gunpowder and had a fuse that was lit just before being thrown. The resulting explosion could cause terrible wounds - often to the user as well as the target.

QUEEN ANNE PISTOL

The barrel of the Queen Anne pistol was unscrewed for loading shot. As battle rarely allowed time for reloading, the shooter needed to make each bullet count. Most pirates were excellent shots and took great care of their pistols - after all, their lives often depended on them.

Common Lead Sho

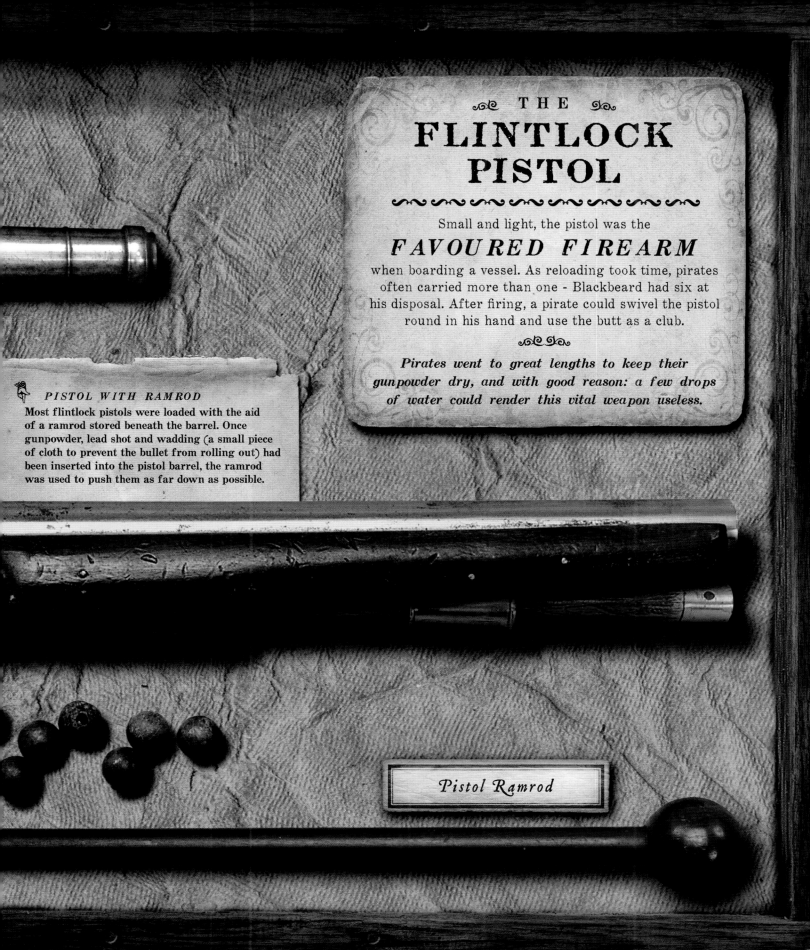

THE
FLINTLOCK PISTOL

Small and light, the pistol was the

FAVOURED FIREARM

when boarding a vessel. As reloading took time, pirates often carried more than one - Blackbeard had six at his disposal. After firing, a pirate could swivel the pistol round in his hand and use the butt as a club.

Pirates went to great lengths to keep their gunpowder dry, and with good reason: a few drops of water could render this vital weapon useless.

PISTOL WITH RAMROD

Most flintlock pistols were loaded with the aid of a ramrod stored beneath the barrel. Once gunpowder, lead shot and wadding (a small piece of cloth to prevent the bullet from rolling out) had been inserted into the pistol barrel, the ramrod was used to push them as far down as possible.

Pistol Ramrod

The Wrecking
of the
Queen Anne's Revenge

A few days after the Charleston blockade, the *Queen Anne's Revenge* ran aground on a sandbar at Beaufort Inlet on the North Carolina coast and was damaged beyond repair. In the chaos that followed, Blackbeard transferred the valuables from the wreck to a smaller vessel and marooned many of his crew on a nearby island. The abandoned men were eventually rescued by the pirate Stede Bonnet.

Lost to the Silent Sea

It is hard to believe that Blackbeard, an exceptional sailor, would have allowed his flagship to end her days thus - unless perhaps he desired it. Could it be that the pirate, realizing that such a large ship and crew had become a burden, deliberately wrecked his vessel so as to break up the company and increase his share of the treasure? There are many who say it is so, though who can know for sure? For it is doubtful that either the mysterious sea or the mighty wreck that lies in her silent depths will ever reveal their dark secrets...

Blackbeard's Lost Treasure

Legends abound as to the whereabouts of Blackbeard's fortune. Some say he buried it at his hideout on Ocracoke Island, perhaps in Teach's Hole, a cove at the island's southern tip. Others believe the treasure was hidden in a stone vault deep beneath the ground at Plum Point, the place where Blackbeard lived for a short time. Still others say Blackbeard left it on the Isle of Shoals in a cave that has long since disappeared under the sea.

But whatever the truth, treasure seekers beware – for legend has it that any who get close to these lost riches will be warned to stay away. Some digging on Ocracoke Island have told of being overcome by a creeping sense of dread, or of hearing ghostly voices – muttered curses and snatches of sea-dog shanties that seem to carry on the winds along this storm-battered coastline. In life, Blackbeard risked his very soul to make his fortune – in death, it seems he may watch over his treasure yet…

What grasping hands have clutched these French gold coins? Is it possible these treasures were removed from Blackbeard's cabin after his death? Dating from the reign of Louis XIV, one is tempted to suppose they fell into Blackbeard's hands when he captured the French Concorde, the ship that became the Queen Anne's Revenge. W. Teach.

Edward Low

Perhaps the most heartless scoundrel ever to sail the seas, Edward Low took cruel pleasure in torturing his captives. It was said that terrible danger lurked in this villain's very smile, for he was as likely to kill a man while in a good humour as he was in a hot-blooded rage.

LOW'S EARLY YEARS WERE SPENT PICK-POCKETING on the streets of London. Tiring of this life, Low travelled to North America and eventually settled in Boston. In 1722, his wife died in childbirth, and he joined a sloop headed for Honduras working as a rigger. One day, after an argument with the captain, the hot-tempered Low fired a musket at the man, narrowly missing him. Low escaped with several crew mates in a small boat, and a day later the men captured a sloop. Raising the black flag, Low "declared war on all the world".

Low took to the pirate life with ease. Prowling the shipping lanes between Boston and New York, he plundered vessels by the dozen. After heading south for the Cayman Islands, Low fell in with the pirate George Lowther and together these rogues attacked ships throughout the West Indies, torturing their victims along the way. Prisoners had their noses and lips hacked off, bodies were torn apart for sport and some were burnt alive.

SWIVEL GUN
Swivel guns were portable cannon that could be positioned where needed to send out a lethal blast of small cannonballs. Pirates could use them to pick off a ship's crew before boarding the vessel.

A Black-Hearted Brute

After a time Low parted company with Lowther, and with a crew of 45 men he continued to build his reputation for senseless cruelty. In a fit of rage he once sliced off a captain's lips and forced the man to eat them. In another barbaric act, Low burnt his cook alive, commenting that he was a "greasy fellow who would fry well". A bounty was placed on Low's head, but reports differ as to how he met his end. Some say his ship sank in a storm with the loss of all hands, while others claim that Low's own men, tired of his savage ways, marooned him on an island. Or perhaps, as some believe, Low sailed off to Brazil where he lived as a free man, never paying the price for his evil deeds.

GRUESOME ENDS

THE YEAR IS 1720, AND ON A STIFLING JUNE AFTERNOON AN AIR OF HUSHED EXPECTATION HOVERS OVER A CROWD GATHERED AT GALLOWS POINT, JAMAICA.

A horse-drawn cart appears, and the onlookers strain to see the prisoner carried aloft. As the cart comes to rest, a chaplain urges the condemned man to repent of his wicked deeds but the pirate only spits with contempt. The hangman places the prisoner's head in a waiting noose and the horse pulls the cart away. Strangled gasps escape from the prisoner's mouth, but death does not come quickly. For though the man's face turns blue and his eyes bulge, his limbs begin to convulse wildly. Yet another pirate is "dancing the devil's jig"...

To be a pirate was a dangerous calling – those lured by the promise of riches well knew the risks. The bodies of executed pirates were frequently hung up in iron cages, where their eyes were pecked out by seagulls and their flesh rotted away. Visible to all, these grisly corpses warned of the terrible fate awaiting those who turned to piracy.

Pirate Justice

During Blackbeard's era, some governors turned a blind eye to the evil that plagued their waters. However, as pirate numbers and crimes increased, so too did the desire to root out these villains. The authorities began hunting down the likes of Blackbeard, Roberts and Rackham – and when such cutthroats fell into the hands of the law, they could expect no mercy...

STEDE BONNET
South Carolinians look on as the pirate Stede Bonnet is hanged at Charleston in December 1718.

WRIST IRONS
Irons were used to restrain imprisoned pirates as they waited to stand trial.

Dancing the Devil's Jig

Captured pirates were imprisoned in dark, rat-infested jails while they awaited trial. If found guilty, they almost certainly faced death by hanging. It became common to execute entire pirate crews – the largest-ever mass hanging took place at Cape Coast Castle in West Africa, where 54 of Bartholomew Roberts' crew were sent to the hangman. Crowds were encouraged to attend pirate executions as a spectacle.

GRIM WARNING
The tarred corpse of the famous English pirate Captain Kidd is displayed in an iron cage as a warning against piracy.

After a chaplain had warned against the evils of piracy, the condemned man was allowed to utter his final words before the noose closed around his neck – some repented, some told jokes and some merely laughed in the face of death. The pirate's body was then cut down and buried in an unmarked grave, or "hung up to dry", the rotting corpse displayed in an iron cage as a grim warning to others.

Ye and each
of your
same adjudged
are sentenced to be
carried back to the Place from whence
you came, from there to the

PLACE OF EXECUTION

without the Gates of this Castle, and there within
the Flood Marks to be hanged by the neck

**TILL YOU ARE DEAD,
DEAD, DEAD.**

And the Lord have Mercy on your Souls

Death sentence passed on the crew of
BARTHOLOMEW ROBERTS,
5 April 1722

Woodes Rogers

Before he was appointed pirate hunter, the English-born Woodes Rogers sailed the world's oceans as a privateer, amassing a fortune in gold and jewels. He plundered foreign merchant ships, attacked a Spanish colony on the Pacific coast, and even captured a Spanish galleon laden with rich treasures.

BOLD, DARING AND WITH A HEART as black as any pirate, Rogers survived mutiny, disease and ferocious storms, not to mention fearsome sea battles. By 1717, he had been made governor of the Bahamas and was charged with ridding the Caribbean of piracy. A pirate in all but name, Rogers knew the tricks of the trade – and so he turned his piratical mind to ruthlessly rooting out the great rogues of the age.

Ruthless Pirate Hunter

Rogers' strategy was to offer pirates a pardon. Hundreds accepted the offer, though many like the scurrilous Jack Rackham soon returned to their wicked ways. The governor's answer was to turn pardoned pirates into pirate hunters. One of these was Benjamin Hornigold, Blackbeard's former captain and friend. This traitor spent the next 18 months cruising the Caribbean to hunt down his old associates, and captured a number who were later hanged. Hornigold was killed when his ship was caught in a hurricane and dashed upon rocks in late 1719. However, Rogers and his men continued their vicious war. When the governor died in 1732, his mission had been accomplished – the cutthroat villains that had long ruled Caribbean waters were no more. Roger's saying "Piracy Expelled, Commerce Restored" remained the Bahamas' motto until the islands gained independence in 1973.

SAILING
THE SEVEN SEAS

Rogers's life before he turned pirate hunter was one of extraordinary adventure. In 1708, the pirate and explorer

WILLIAM DAMPIER

- a skilled navigator who had already circled the globe twice - approached Rogers to lead a privateering voyage. In three years the men sailed around the world boldly attacking Spanish shipping and capturing many prizes. Perhaps their most notable exploit, though, was the rescue of Alexander Selkirk, a Scot who had been marooned on an uninhabited island in the Pacific Ocean for over four years.

Selkirk's extraordinary tale of survival was to form the basis for Daniel Defoe's classic novel, *Robinson Crusoe*.

William Dampier

Blackbeard's Last Battle

After the wrecking of the *Queen Anne's Revenge*, Blackbeard returned to his lair on Ocracoke Island. In October 1718 he threw a wild party that lasted for days. Although the North Carolina governor Charles Eden tolerated Blackbeard's presence – many say he was bribed with stolen goods – Governor Spotswood of Virginia decided the time had come to get rid of this villainous rogue once and for all.

Blackbeard Hunted Down

Spotswood hired two vessels and manned them with 57 sailors under the command of Lieutenant Maynard. On 21 November Maynard tracked down Blackbeard's sloop *Adventure* at Ocracoke Island. Half of Blackbeard's crew were ashore in nearby Bath Town and realizing he was in trouble, Blackbeard fired grapeshot at the two vessels. A good many men were killed, but return fire forced *Adventure* to run aground on a sandbank.

Maynard had hidden many of his men in the holds. Blackbeard, seeing only dead men strewn across the decks, decided to board. With bloodthirsty cries he and his pirates leapt on deck only to be met by Maynard's crew bursting from below. After pistol fire, Blackbeard drew his cutlass and with a single stroke of brute strength broke Maynard's sword. However, the lieutenant's men surrounded the pirate, inflicting numerous wounds to his back and slashing him across the neck. Fighting till his great frame could take no more, Blackbeard eventually crashed to the deck. The "king of pyrates" was dead...

A Gruesome Trophy

Maynard hacked off Blackbeard's head, and hung his grisly prize from the bowsprit of his sloop. As for the survivors and those crew members who had been ashore, they were rounded up and taken to Williamsburg, Virginia to stand trial. Israel Hands escaped the hangman's noose – it is claimed he testified against his fellow pirates in exchange for his freedom. In March 1719, his 13 crew mates were hanged in Williamsburg and their rotting corpses hung in iron cages along Gallows Road.

Blackbeard Lives On

There are those who say Blackbeard's tormented spirit haunts the North Carolina coastline. Now and again, when a violent gale howls across the water, and the waves crash in a seething mass of foam, strange glowing lights can be seen across the sea. Many have testified to seeing a ball of fire crossing the water from Plum Point, a place where Blackbeard once briefly lived. This fireball never deviates from its straight course, even when the wind rages with all its might...

United in Death

After Blackbeard's head was cut off, it was placed on a pole at the entrance to Norfolk, Virginia as a grim warning to other pirates. Yet one black and stormy night, the skull disappeared without a trace. As to its fate, who can know for sure? Some say it was taken by fellow pirates, "bretheren of the coast", and fashioned into a silver-plated punch bowl that survives to this day. Still others claim it was Blackbeard's ghost that removed the skull and carried it off to the murky depths of the sea near Beaufort Inlet, North Carolina, where the wreck of the *Queen Anne's Revenge* is said to lie in shifting sands. Perhaps the skull lies there still, a pirate and his ship united in their dark and watery grave for ever more...

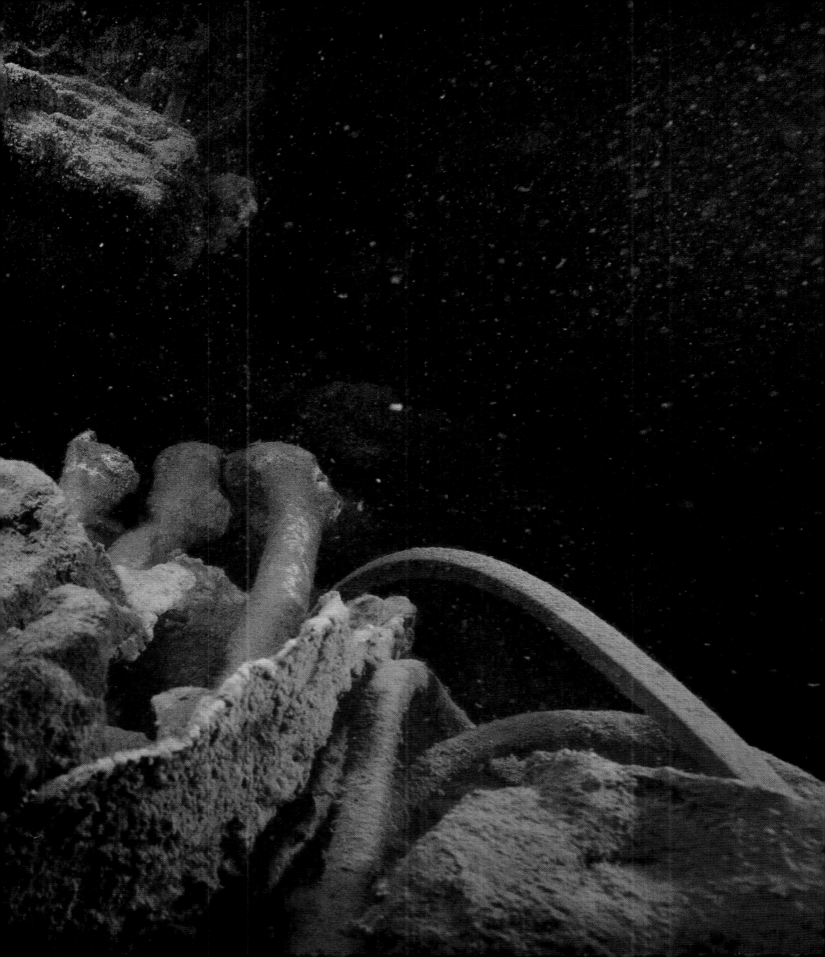

Acknowledgements

350 · 1238

Published in 2015 by Carlton Books Limited
An imprint of the Carlton Publishing Group
20 Mortimer Street, London W1T 3JW

10 9 8 7 6 5 4 3 2 1

A catalogue record for this book is available from the British Library.

ISBN: 978-1-78312-116-8

Printed in China

Picture Credits:

The publishers would like to thank the following sources for their kind permission to reproduce the pictures in this book.

Key: t: top, b: bottom, l: left, r: right.
Akg-Images: 35. Alamy Images: /Imagebroker: 7tr, 17. Ancient Art & Architecture: 48bc. Bridgeman Art Library: 32-33, /Howard Pyle /American Illustrators Gallery: 45br, /Giraudon: 37b, /English School /Peter Newark American Pictures: 56, /Michael Graham-Stewart: 70b. Corbis: /Bettmann: 74-75, /Tria Giovan: 10-11, 39, 58-59b. DK Images: 7br, 48-49, 65, 70l. Dover Publishing: 15, 57b, 73. Getty Images: /English School: 28-29, 34tl, 34br, /Lorentz Gullachsen: 4-5, /Arnulf Husmo: 2-3, 41, /Oxford Scientific /Photolibrary: 76-77, /Brian Skerry: 78-79, /Stephen St. John: 37l. IStockphoto: 38r, 45l, 69, 71. Mary Evans Picture Library: 44. National Maritime Museum: 20, 21tl, 21tr, 21br, 29, 31-32, 34c, 36, 48-49c, 51, 57b, 57c, 58-59b, 58-59c, 58-59t, 60c, 61. Picture Desk: 46, /Gianni Dagli Orti: 7b, 38b, 48tl, 64-65b, /Jean Vinchon Numismatist Paris /Gianni Dagli Orti: 7b, 38b, 64-65b. Private Collection: 29r, 71c. Royal Armouries Museum: 67-68. Sanders, Oxford: 12-13, 30-31. Science & Society: /Science Museum: 7l, 30, 41r. Stock.XCHNG: 36-37, 46br. Topfoto.co.uk: 6-7, 47, 60t.

Every effort has been made to acknowledge correctly and contact the source and/or copyright holder of each picture and Carlton Books Limited apologizes for any unintentional errors or omissions, which will be corrected in future editions of this book.

The author would like to express his sincere gratitude to the following:

MY LONG-SUFFERING FAMILY, for their unwavering encouragement; the publisher, for having the courage to believe; *Stella Caldwell*, my colleague and writing assistant; *Barry Timms*, for his editorial guidance and critical insight; *Russell Porter* and *Drew McGovern*, for their fine design work; *Frank DeNota* for his superb digital artworks, *Leo Brown* for his wonderful character drawings, and *Jon Lucas* and *Dud Moseley* for their illustrations; *Ben White* for picture research; *Claire Halligan* for production; and finally, *Benjamin Hands* – wherever he may be – without whose generosity of spirit, this book would never have been started.